Martin Luther King Jr.

by Lola M. Schaefer

Consulting Editor:
Gail Saunders-Smith, Ph.D.

Consultant:
Mirma A. Johnson,
Curator of Education
National Civil Rights Museum

Pebble Books

an imprint of Capstone Press
Mankato, Minnesota

Handwritten annotations: MARIE — 443-912-4679

W9-DIP-037

8ve 579-6141

Smau $Incyen

Pebble Books are published by Capstone Press
1710 Roe Crest Drive, North Mankato, Minnesota 56003
www.capstonepub.com

Library of Congress Cataloging-in-Publication Data
Schaefer, Lola M., 1950–
    Martin Luther King, Jr./by Lola M. Schaefer.
        p. cm.—(Famous Americans)
    Includes bibliographical references and index.
    Summary: Photographs and simple text provide an introduction to the life of Dr. Martin
Luther King.
    ISBN-13: 978-0-7368-0111-9 (hardcover)
    ISBN-10: 0-7368-0111-1 (hardcover)
    ISBN-13: 978-0-7368-8112-8 (softcover)
    ISBN-10: 0-7368-8112-3 (softcover)
    1. King, Martin Luther, Jr., 1929–1968—Juvenile literature. 2. Afro-Americans—Biography—
Juvenile literature. 3. Civil rights workers—United States—Biography—Juvenile literature.
4. Baptists—United States—Clergy—Biography—Juvenile literature. [1. King, Martin Luther, Jr.,
1929–1968. 2. Civil rights workers. 3. Clergy. 4. Afro-Americans—Biography.] I. Title. II. Series.
E185.97.K5S3 1999
323'.092—dc21   98-19960
[B]   CIP
                                                                              AC

Note to Parents and Teachers

This series supports national history standards by providing easy-to-read
biographies of people who had a great impact on history. This book describes
and illustrates the life of Dr. Martin Luther King, Jr., a civil rights leader in the
1950s and 1960s. The photographs support early readers in understanding the
text. Repetition of words and phrases helps early readers learn new words. This
book introduces early readers to vocabulary used in this subject area. The
vocabulary is defined in the Words to Know section. Early readers may need
assistance in reading some words and in using the Table of Contents, Words to
Know, Read More, Internet Sites, and Index/Word List sections of the book.

Printed in the United States of America in North Mankato, Minnesota.
062013   007365R

Table of Contents

Martin Luther King, Jr., was born in Georgia on January 15, 1929. Martin was African American. His father was a minister of a church. Martin's father taught him to accept all people.

Martin and his family liked people of all races. Not all white people and African American people liked each other. Some people wanted segregation. Segregation separated people because of the color of their skin.

8

Martin learned that front seats on buses were for white people only. Back seats on buses were for African American people only. Martin did not like segregation. He wanted all people to be treated the same.

Martin went to college to become a minister. He read about strong, peaceful people. These people made changes in their countries. Martin wanted to make peaceful changes for African American people.

Martin became a minister in 1948. Martin met and married Coretta Scott. They moved to Alabama. Martin led a church. He preached that all people should be treated the same.

Martin started many groups to help African American people. He knew segregation laws could be changed. He helped African American people plan peaceful meetings. He told them changes would come slowly.

Martin led African American people in peaceful marches. The country watched. He gave powerful speeches. The country listened. Some people liked his ideas.

Courts heard cases about segregation laws. The courts said segregation was wrong. New laws ended segregation. The laws gave African American people the same rights as white people. The laws said all people must be treated the same.

Martin Luther King, Jr., won the Nobel Peace Prize in 1964. The prize honored Martin for his peaceful work. Martin was killed on April 4, 1968. Today people celebrate Martin Luther King, Jr., Day in January.

Words to Know

African American—a citizen of the United States with an African background

college—a place where students study after high school

court—a place where legal cases are heard and decided

minister—a person who leads a church

Nobel Peace Prize—an award given to a person who helps bring about peace

preach—to give a religious talk to people, especially during a church service

segregation—the act of separating people because of the color of their skin

Read More

Bray, Rosemary L. *Martin Luther King.* New York: Greenwillow Books, 1995.

Frost, Helen. *Martin Luther King, Jr. Day.* National Holidays. Mankato, Minn.: Pebble Books, 2000.

Lazo, Caroline. *Martin Luther King, Jr.* Peacemakers. New York: Dillon Press, 1994.

Strazzabosco, Jeanne. *Learning about Dignity from the Life of Martin Luther King, Jr.* A Character Building Book. New York: PowerKids Press, 1996.

Internet Sites

FactHound offers a safe, fun way to find Internet sites related to this book.

Go to *www.facthound.com*
Type in this code: 0736801111

He'll fetch the best sites for you!

Index/Word List

Word Count: 291
Early-Intervention Level: 24

Editorial Credits
Michelle L. Norstad, editor; Clay Schotzko/Icon Productions, cover designer;
  Sheri Gosewisch, photo researcher

Photo Credits
AP/Wide World Photos, 12
Archive Photos, cover, 4, 10, 14, 16, 20
Photo Network/MacDonald Photography, 18
UPI/Corbis-Bettmann, 1, 6, 8